The Prince of
Peace

The Prince of
Peace

Russell M. Nelson

Deseret Book

Salt Lake City, Utah

Design © 2016 Deseret Book Company
Art direction by Richard Erickson
Design by Sheryl Dickert Smith
Front and back cover wreath and pine boughs, Shutterstock / © Eisfrei
Interior embellishments, Shutterstock / © Eisfrei, © Yudina Anna,
  © Kastovsky, © Jane_Lane

© 2016 Russell M. Nelson

All rights reserved. No part of this book may be reproduced in any form or by any means without permission in writing from the publisher, Deseret Book Company, at permissions@deseretbook.com or P. O. Box 30178, Salt Lake City, Utah 84130. This work is not an official publication of The Church of Jesus Christ of Latter-day Saints. The views expressed herein are the responsibility of the author and do not necessarily represent the position of the Church or of Deseret Book Company.

DESERET BOOK is a registered trademark of Deseret Book Company.

Visit us at DeseretBook.com

ISBN 978-1-62972-283-2

Printed in the United States of America
Artistic Printing, Salt Lake City, UT

10 9 8 7 6 5 4 3 2

Memories of Christmas bring recollections of family, of gifts, and of service to others. They stem from the real reason for Christmas, that transcendent gift from our Heavenly Father: "For God so loved the world, that he gave his only begotten Son, that whosoever believeth in him should not perish, but have everlasting life."[1]

Focusing on the Lord and everlasting life can help us not only at Christmas but through all the challenges of mortality. Imperfect people share Planet Earth with other imperfect people. Ours is a fallen world marred by excessive debt, wars, natural disasters, disease, and death.

RUSSELL M. NELSON

Personal challenges come. A father may have lost his job. A young mother may have learned of a grave illness. A son or a daughter may have gone astray. Whatever may cause the worry, each of us yearns to find inner peace.

My message pertains to the only source of true and lasting peace: Jesus the Christ—the Prince of Peace.[2] This title He bore in addition to others for which He was foreordained.

He was anointed by His Father to be the Savior of the world. These two titles—the Messiah, and the Christ—designated His responsibility as the *anointed one*.[3]

Under the direction of His Father, Jesus was Creator of this and other worlds.[4] Jesus is our Advocate with the Father.[5] Jesus was the promised Immanuel,[6] the great I Am and Jehovah of Old Testament times.[7]

He was sent by His Father to accomplish the Atonement, *the* central act of all human history.

Jesus is our Advocate with the Father. Jesus was the promised Immanuel, the great I Am and Jehovah of Old Testament times.

Because of His Atonement, immortality became a reality for all, and eternal life became a possibility for those who choose to follow Him.[8] These objectives are the work and glory of Almighty God.[9]

As our great Exemplar, Jesus taught us how to live, to love, and to learn. He taught us how to pray, forgive, and endure to the end.[10] He taught us how to care about others more than we care about ourselves. He taught us about mercy and kindness—making real changes in our lives through His power. He taught us how to find peace of heart and mind. One day, we will stand before Him as our just Judge and merciful Master.[11]

These sacred responsibilities of the Lord cause us to adore Him as the personal and perennial Prince of Peace.

He can bring peace to those whose lives have been ravaged by war. Families disrupted by military duty bear memories of war, which in my mind were imbedded during the Korean War. Wars of our present era are more sophisticated, but they are still as wrenching to families. Those who so suffer can turn to the Lord. His is the consoling message of peace on earth and goodwill among men.[12]

Peace can come to those who are not feeling well. Some have bodies that are wounded. Others ache spiritually because of missing loved ones or other emotional trauma. Brothers and sisters, peace can come to your soul as you build faith in the Prince of Peace.

"Have ye any that are sick among you? Bring them hither. Have ye any that are lame, or blind, or halt, or maimed, . . . or that are afflicted in any manner? Bring them hither and I will heal them."[13]

"I see that your faith is sufficient that I should heal you."[14]

Peace can come to one who suffers in sorrow. If by chance that sorrow stems from a mistake or a sin, all the Lord requires is real repentance. Scripture pleads with us to "flee [from] youthful lusts; . . . [and] call on the Lord out of a pure heart."[15] Then His soothing "balm in Gilead" can heal even a sin-sick soul.[16]

Think of the change in John Newton, born in London in 1725. He repented of his sinful life as a slave-trader to become an Anglican clergyman. With that mighty change of heart, John wrote words to the hymn "Amazing Grace":

> *Amazing grace! How sweet the sound*
> *That saved a wretch like me.*
> *I once was lost, but now am found,*
> *Was blind, but now I see.*[17]

"Joy shall be in heaven over one sinner that repenteth."[18]

Peace can come to those whose labors are heavy: "Come unto me, all ye that labour and are heavy laden, and I will give you rest.

"Take my yoke upon you, and learn of me; for I

The Prince of Peace

am meek and lowly in heart: and ye shall find rest unto your souls.

"For my yoke is easy, and my burden is light."[19]

Peace can come to those who mourn. The Lord said, "Blessed are they that mourn: for they shall be comforted."[20] As we endure the passing of a loved one, we can be filled with the peace of the Lord through the whisperings of the Spirit.

"Those that die in me shall not taste of death, for it shall be sweet unto them."[21]

"Peace I leave with you, my peace I give unto you: not as the world giveth, give I unto you. Let not your heart be troubled, neither let it be afraid."[22]

"I am the resurrection, and the life: he that believeth in me, though he were dead, yet shall he live:

"And whosoever liveth and believeth in me shall never die."[23]

Peace can come to all who earnestly seek the Prince of Peace. His is the sweet and saving message our

Peace can come to all

who choose to walk in the

ways of the Master.

His invitation is expressed

in three loving words:

"Come, follow me."

missionaries take throughout the world. They preach the gospel of Jesus Christ as restored by Him through the Prophet Joseph Smith.[24] Missionaries teach these life-changing words of the Lord: "If ye love me, keep my commandments."[25]

Peace can come to all who choose to walk in the ways of the Master. His invitation is expressed in three loving words: "Come, follow me."[26]

We'll sing all hail to the Prince of Peace![27] For He will come again. Then "the glory of the Lord shall be revealed, and all flesh shall see it together."[28] As the Millennial Messiah, He will reign as King of kings and Lord of lords.[29]

As we follow Jesus Christ, He will lead us to live with Him and our Heavenly Father, along with our families. Through our many challenges of mortality, if we remain faithful to covenants made, if we endure to the end, we will qualify for that greatest of all the gifts of God, eternal life.³⁰ In His holy presence, our families can be together forever.

God bless you, my dear brothers and sisters. May you and your loved ones enjoy forever all the blessings of our Lord—the Prince of Peace.

Notes

1. John 3:16.
2. Isaiah 9:6; 2 Nephi 19:6.
3. *Messiah* in Hebrew and *Christ* in Greek both mean "anointed."
4. See Moses 1:32–33.
5. See 1 John 2:1; Doctrine and Covenants 29:5; 110:4.
6. See Isaiah 7:14; 2 Nephi 17:14; Matthew 1:23.
7. See Abraham 1:16; 2:8; Exodus 3:11–14; 6:3.
8. See 3 Nephi 27:13–14.
9. See Moses 1:39.
10. See 3 Nephi 27:21.
11. See 2 Nephi 9:41.
12. See Luke 2:14.
13. 3 Nephi 17:7.
14. 3 Nephi 17:8; see also Matthew 13:15; 3 Nephi 18:32; Doctrine and Covenants 112:13.
15. 2 Timothy 2:22; see also 3 Nephi 9:13.
16. Jeremiah 8:22; see also "There Is a Balm in Gilead," attributed to Washington Glass (1854).
17. John Newton, *Olney Hymns* (1779); see also John 9:25.
18. Luke 15:7; see also 15:10.
19. Matthew 11:28–30.
20. Matthew 5:4; see also 3 Nephi 12:4; Doctrine and Covenants 101:14.
21. Doctrine and Covenants 42:46.
22. John 14:27.

Notes

23. John 11:25–26.
24. We also remember the birthday of the Prophet Joseph Smith (December 23, 1805) at Christmastime.
25. John 14:15.
26. Luke 18:22.
27. See "We'll Sing All Hail to Jesus' Name," *Hymns of The Church of Jesus Christ of Latter-day Saints* (1985), 182.
28. Isaiah 40:5.
29. See Revelation 19:16.
30. See Doctrine and Covenants 14:7.